Matter and Material

By Darlene R. Stille

THE CHILD'S WORLD®
CHANHASSEN, MINNESOTA

The Child's World

Published in the United States of America by The Child's World®
PO Box 326, Chanhassen, MN 55317-0326
800-599-READ
www.childsworld.com

Content Adviser:
Mats Selen, PhD,
Professor of Physics,
University of Illinois,
Urbana, Illinois

Photo Credits: Cover: Cover: A. Pasieka/Photo Researchers.
Interior: Bettmann/Corbis: 4, 30-top, 30-bottom; Corbis: 7 (Archivo Iconografico,
S.A.) 8, 11 (Lester V. Bergman), 12, 13 (Lester Lefkowitz), 14 (Macduff Everton), 15, 16
(LWA-Dann Tardif), 19, 21 (Richard Hamilton Smith), 22 (Wolfgang Kaehler), 25, 26
(Ted Horowitz), 30-middle; Getty Images: 17 (The Image Bank/Jody Dole), 18
(NASA/Newsmakers); PictureQuest: 9 (Don Farrall/Photodisc), 24 (Don
Kreuter/Rainbow); Dave Spier/Visuals Unlimited: 5.

The Child's World®: Mary Berendes, Publishing Director

Editorial Directions, Inc.: E. Russell Primm, Editorial Director; Pam Rosenberg, Line
Editor; Katie Marsico, Assistant Editor; Matt Messbarger, Editorial Assistant; Susan
Hindman, Copy Editor; Susan Ashley, Proofreader; Peter Garnham, Olivia Nellums, and
Katherine Trickle, Fact Checkers; Tim Griffin/IndexServ, Indexer; Cian Laughlin O'Day,
Photo Researcher; Linda S. Koutris, Photo Selector

The Design Lab: Kathleen Petelinsek, Design; Kari Thornborough, Page Production

Library of Congress Cataloging-in-Publication Data
Stille, Darlene R.
  Matter and material / by Darlene R. Stille.
     v. cm.— (Science around us)
Includes bibliographical references and index.
Contents: Discovering matter—Basic stuff : atoms, elements, and molecules—What's
that stuff? physical and chemical properties of matter—Knowing your stuff : raw and
manufactured materials and elements and compounds—Picking the right stuff : proper-
ties of materials—Making new stuff : physical and chemical changes.
  ISBN 1-59296-223-8 (lib. bdg. : alk. paper) 1. Matter—Juvenile literature. [1. Matter.]
I. Title. II. Science around us (Child's World (Firm))
  QC173.16.S75 2005
  530—dc22   2003027227

TABLE OF CONTENTS

CHAPTER ONE

DISCOVERING MATTER

No one can say who discovered matter. It is impossible even to say who thought about it first. Matter is everywhere. Matter is all the stuff in the **universe.** Everything that you can see, touch, taste, feel, or smell is made of matter.

Prehistoric people probably did not think about matter. They were busy hunting for food, running from wild animals, and keeping warm and dry. They learned how to change matter to make life better, but they did not know that they were changing matter. They changed matter to make fire. They burned sticks of wood and changed

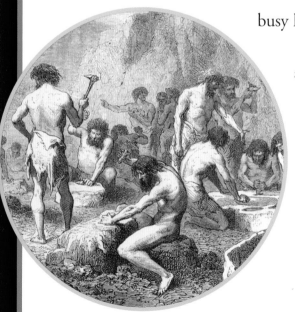

Prehistoric people learned how to change matter to make tools and cook food.

Fire can be used to change matter.

them into piles of ashes. Later, they used fire to change matter. They

heated certain rocks called **ores** with fire. They were able to get

iron and other **metals** out of these heated ores. Weapons and tools

were made from these metals.

We know the ancient Greeks thought about matter. They wondered what all the stuff around them was made of. Thousands of years ago, they came up with the idea of **atoms.** They said that everything in the world is made of hard little parts called atoms. They were getting close to discovering the nature of matter.

In the 1600s and 1700s, scientists in Europe were thinking about matter in another way. They said that matter has different forms. They called these forms "states of matter." They named the ordinary states of matter **solids, liquids,** and **gases.**

They learned that solids have a shape. A solid always takes up the same amount of space.

They learned that liquids have no shape. A liquid takes the shape of whatever container it is in. But a liquid always takes up the same amount of space. A measuring cup full of water takes up the same

Democritus was an ancient Greek philosopher who came up with the idea that all matter was made up of basic particles that he called atoms.

Helium is a gas that weighs less than the mixture of gases that make up the air we breath. That is why it is used to fill balloons and make them float in air.

amount of space whether it is poured into a drinking glass or a bowl.

They learned that gases have no shape. A gas never takes up the same amount of space. A gas goes outward to fill any container that it is in. The same amount of gas will fill a small balloon or a big tank. Scientists also learned that a gas has **weight.**

Today, we know that matter is all the stuff in the universe. Anything that takes up space is matter. Even the air you breathe is made of matter.

The ancient Greeks asked, What is matter made of, and what is the most basic stuff in the universe? Scientists think they have answered these questions.

CHAPTER TWO

BASIC STUFF

The ancient Greeks were on the right track. All the stuff in the universe is made of atoms. Atoms are tiny bits of matter much too small for you to see.

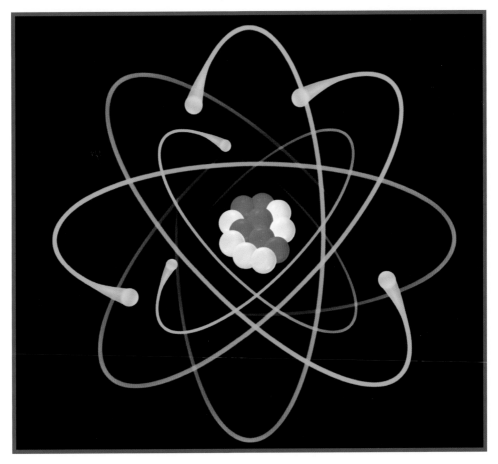

Scientists today know that atoms have a positively charged nucleus and negatively charged electrons that move around the nucleus.

How small is an atom? Take a look at one hair. What if you could slice that hair like you would slice a sausage? Imagine taking that thin slice of hair and chopping it into billions of pieces. Each piece would still contain several atoms. Atoms are the building blocks of matter.

Imagine having a set of 91 different kinds of blocks that you could put together to make anything in the world. What would you call those blocks?

In nature, there are 91 basic building blocks. Scientists call them chemical elements. These building blocks are actually 91 different kinds of atoms, one for each naturally occurring element.

Each chemical element is made of one type of atom. Iron atoms make iron. Oxygen atoms make oxygen. Hydrogen atoms make hydrogen gas. Iron, oxygen, and hydrogen are three chemical elements.

These strands of human hair have been magnified 100 times. You would have to chop each of these hairs into billions of pieces before you would even come close to having a piece that contained just one atom!

Atoms can fit together to make other building blocks called

molecules. Some molecules are made of only one kind of

atom. Some molecules are made of many different kinds of atoms.

Atoms and molecules join together in millions of different

ways. They join to make the food

you eat. They join to

make your skin and

hair. They join to

make the water

you drink and

the air you

breathe. They join

to make everything

in the universe.

*The water you drink is made up of atoms of hydrogen
and oxygen joined together to make a molecules of water.*

A car and a locomotive are speeding along at 100 kilometers (60 miles) an hour. Which can stop faster? The answer depends on three things—inertia, mass, and force.

Both the car and the locomotive have something called inertia. Inertia makes the car and the locomotive keep on doing whatever they are doing. If the car and the locomotive are standing still, inertia keeps them standing still. If the car and the locomotive are moving, inertia keeps them moving.

That might sound like the car and the locomotive are lazy. But everything made of matter has inertia. Inertia is a property of matter.

The locomotive is much bigger than the car. Physicists say the locomotive has more mass than the car. Mass is the amount of matter in something. The locomotive is made of a lot more matter than the car.

The more mass an object has, the greater its inertia. The drivers of the car and the locomotive have to apply a force to overcome inertia. They both use the force of brakes. The brakes slow the turning wheels.

The more mass something has, the harder it is to change its speed. If both drivers use the same amount of braking force, it will take the locomotive much longer to stop. If the locomotive driver applies a lot more braking force, the locomotive will stop in the same time as the car.

CHAPTER THREE

WHAT'S THAT STUFF?

With all those atoms and molecules around, the world

could be a confusing place. But there are ways to sort all

the things that you encounter in daily life. You know you can sort

matter into solids, liquids, and gases. But when it comes to liquids,

Rocks are solid, water is a liquid, and the air around them is a mixture of gases. All of the matter around you can be sorted into these three categories.

exactly why do you know the difference between liquids such as milk and orange juice? You know because you use your five senses to tell them apart.

You can tell what

How do you know that these are oranges and that there is orange juice in the glass? You use your five senses to find out if they look, taste, and smell like oranges.

something is by sight, smell, touch, taste, or hearing. You can use your senses because matter has **properties.** Properties are like ID tags on matter. Color, taste, and smell are some of the physical properties that identify matter.

Line up three glasses with water, milk, and orange juice. Look at their color. Water is clear, milk is white, and orange juice is orange.

A pillow filled with feathers is light enough to be picked up and played with because the matter in feathers is not dense.

Put on a blindfold and smell the glasses of liquid. Each has its own smell. Stay blindfolded and take a sip from each glass. Water, milk, and orange juice taste very different from one another.

There are many other properties that you can look for. Density tells how much matter is packed into something. A bag of feathers weighs much less than the same size bag of iron balls. Feathers are less dense than iron.

Solubility is a property that tells whether a solid will dissolve, or disappear, in a liquid. Put a teaspoon of table salt in a big glass of water. Put a teaspoon of sand in another glass of water. Stir up the water in both glasses. The salt grains disappear in the water. The sand drops to the bottom of the glass. Salt is soluble in water. Sand is not.

Some things, like this antacid tablet, are made so that they will dissolve in water.

Some materials are natural, or raw, materials. Some materials are manufactured, or made, from raw materials. Stone, wood, cotton, and leather are raw materials. Iron ore is a raw material taken from the earth. Iron, the metal, is a manufactured material made from iron ore.

Let's go back to your set of 91 blocks. Imagine that one kind of building block is red. Put a bunch of red building blocks together and you have something that is pure red.

Some materials are like that. They are made of only one kind of building block or atom. Atoms of the same kind join to make a molecule. Molecules made of just one kind of atom are called chemical elements. The iron that makes up an iron bar is a chemical element. It is only made of iron atoms.

Your 91 building blocks come in 91 different colors. You can put your blocks together to make things that are only red or green

Cotton is a raw material that grows on cotton plants.

Plastic is a manufactured material that can be made in many different colors.

or yellow or blue. You can also put them together to make things that have more than one color.

Most materials are like that. They are made of many different kinds of atoms joined together to make molecules. Molecules made of different kinds of atoms are called chemical compounds.

You are surrounded by things that are made of more than one kind of atom. Most stuff around you is made of chemical compounds. Wood is a natural material made of chemical compounds. **Plastic** is a manufactured material made of chemical compounds.

CHAPTER FIVE

PICKING THE RIGHT STUFF

Just because all materials are solid doesn't mean all materials can be used for the same tasks. Paper is a solid, but you would never use paper to build a house. Wood is a solid, but you would never print a book on wooden boards. You wouldn't make a beach ball out of glass. You wouldn't make a window out of rubber.

How do you know what kind of material you need to do a job? You test the properties of the material. All matter has properties that tell you what it is. All materials have properties that tell you what they can do.

How strong is a material? Will it bend? Glass can break easily and doesn't bend much. Metal wire is strong and bends easily. You would make a paper clip out of wire but not out of glass.

How long will a material last outdoors? Newspaper turns to mush when it gets wet. Brick can last for thousands of years.

Will electricity go through a material? Electricity goes through copper and other metals. Electricity does not go through wood or plastic. That is why electric wires are made of metal.

Can heat go easily through a material? Heat travels through iron and other metals. That is why cooking pots are made of metal.

Can you see through a material? You can see through clear glass. You cannot see through aluminum foil. That is why windows are made of glass and not aluminum foil.

Bricks can last outdoors for thousands of years, long after the other parts of a building have crumbled and decayed.

Astronomers think there is a kind of matter in the universe that you cannot see, hear, taste, or smell. They call it dark matter.

Scientists learned that something is out there by studying galaxies. Galaxies are made up of trillions of stars. The stars orbit, or go around, the center of a galaxy. By studying how these stars move, scientists can tell that there must be more matter in galaxies than astronomers can see with telescopes. Some kind of mysterious matter is helping to hold the galaxies together. In fact, there might be ten times more dark matter than the regular kind of matter that we can see.

Astronomers are trying to figure out what dark matter could be. It might be huge balls of invisible gas. It might be tiny particles much smaller than an atom. It might be something too strange to imagine.

CHAPTER SIX

MAKING NEW STUFF

Remember how prehistoric people changed matter to make fire and iron? There are two ways that matter can change—physical change and chemical change.

Matter can change from one state to another. During a process often called melting, a solid can change into a liquid. During a process often called boiling, a liquid can change into a gas. Changing from a solid to a liquid or from a liquid to a gas is called a physical change.

You can make water change this way. Put an ice

Scientists are always searching for new ways to change matter and make life better.

cube tray filled with liquid water into your freezer. The water turns into solid ice. Then leave the ice cubes in the kitchen sink. The ice melts and becomes liquid water again. The basic stuff that makes water did not change. It just changed the way it looks.

You can burn a piece of wood. The wood changes into gray ashes. However, you cannot change the ashes back into wood. The wood changed into new stuff when it burned. This kind of change is called a chemical change.

Scientists and engineers use chemical changes to make all kinds of new stuff. They mix elements and compounds to make new kinds of molecules. They mix metals to make new metals that are as light as a feather. They make plastics that are as strong as steel.

Prehistoric people changed matter to make their lives better. People today still change matter to make life better.

GLOSSARY

atoms (AT-uhms) Atoms are tiny bits of matter that are too small to see.

gases (GAS-es) Gases are a form of matter that has no shape or volume.

liquids (LIK-widz) Liquids are a form of matter that has no shape but that does have volume.

metals (MET-uhls) Metals are materials that are usually shiny and hard, and conduct electricity and heat.

molecules (MOL-uh-kyools) Molecules are building blocks of matter made up of more than one atom.

ores (ORS) Ores are rocks that contain metal.

plastic (PLAS-tik) Plastic is a manufactured material that is strong and lightweight and can be molded into different shapes.

properties (PROP-ur-tees) Properties are qualities that help identify matter and materials.

solids (SOL-idz) Solids are a form of matter that has shape and volume.

universe (YOO-nuh-vurss) The universe is everything that exists in space, including Earth, the other planets, and the stars.

weight (WATE) Weight is the measure of the force of gravity pulling on a body.

DID YOU KNOW?

▶ A space that has no matter is called a perfect vacuum. There really is no such thing because there is some matter everywhere in the universe. Even in outer space, far away from stars and planets, there are atoms here and there.

▶ Why can you smell flowers, perfume, and dinner cooking? Atoms and molecules from the flowers, perfume, and food go into the air. They float into your nose. You can't see atoms or molecules, but you can smell them!

▶ There is a fourth state of matter called plasma. Plasma comes from electricity going through gas. You see plasmas all the time. Fluorescent light tubes contain plasmas. Colorful signs light up when electricity goes through neon gas inside thin glass tubes.

▶ There are only 91 natural chemical elements found on Earth, but physicists have learned how to make more elements. They make the new elements in big machines called atom smashers or particle accelerators. They have made at least 18 of these artificial elements. Some physicists claim they have made three more.

▶ Look closely at the surface of still water. The water looks like it has a skin on top. This "skin" is called surface tension. Surface tension lets water spiders and other bugs walk on top of the water.

▶ Gases have different properties of color and smell. You cannot see or smell the gases in air. Other gases have color and odor. Chlorine gas looks like a yellow-green cloud. Hydrogen sulfide gas smells like rotten eggs.

▶ The engine in your family car was once a runny liquid. Red-hot melted iron gets poured into a mold with the shape of a car engine. When the iron cools, it becomes a solid again. The iron has become an auto engine. Many solid metal parts come from liquid metals poured into molds.

▶ Many solids can turn into liquids if they get hot enough. Even solid rocks can melt in the hot, inner part of Earth. Melted rock can pour out of a volcano like a river of fire. The melted rock is called lava.

▶ Oxygen is an important gas in air. All animals need oxygen to live. Oxygen that is made very cold and squeezed into metal bottles turns into a liquid.

TIMELINE

8000 B.C.   The earliest known use of the element copper by ancient civilizations.

3500   The earliest known use of the element iron by ancient people.

400   The ancient Greeks come up with the idea that matter consists of small bits that cannot be broken apart, and they call these tiny bits of matter atoms.

A.D. 1755   Joseph Black (top left) discovers carbon dioxide, a gas.

1774   Joseph Priestley discovers oxygen.

1803   Scientist John Dalton develops his atomic theory, which becomes the basis of all modern atomic science.

1811   Amadeo Avogadro demonstrates the relationship between the volume of a substance and the number of molecules it contains.

1823   Michael Faraday (right), a British scientist, turns chlorine gas into a liquid. His experiment is one of the first successful attempts to liquefy a gas.

1869   Russian chemist Dmitry Mendeleyev publishes his Periodic Table of the Elements, a chart organizing all the elements known at the time according to their properties.

1937   Technetium, the first human-made element, is created by scientists Carlo Perrier and Emilio Segrè (bottom left).

HOW TO LEARN MORE
ABOUT MATTER AND MATERIAL

At the Library

Nardo, Don. *Atoms.* San Diego: Kidhaven, 2001.

Oxlade, Chris. *Metals.* Chicago: Heinemann Library, 2003.

Zoehfeld, Kathleen Weidner, and Paul Meisel (illustrator). *What Is the World Made Of? All about Solids, Liquids, and Gases.* New York: HarperTrophy, 1998.

On the Web

VISIT OUR HOME PAGE FOR LOTS OF LINKS ABOUT MATTER AND MATERIAL:

http://www.childsworld.com/links.html

Note to Parents, Teachers, and Librarians: We routinely verify our Web links to make sure they're safe, active sites—so encourage your readers to check them out!

Places to Visit or Contact

NATIONAL ATOMIC MUSEUM
*To learn more about atoms and
the history of nuclear science*
1905 Mountain Road NW
Albuquerque, NM 87104
505/245-2137

MIAMI MUSEUM OF SCIENCE
*To tour the Atoms Family exhibit
and learn more about matter*
3280 South Miami Avenue
Miami, FL 33129
305/646-4200

INDEX

About the Author

Darlene R. Stille is a science writer. She has lived in Chicago, Illinois, all her life. When she was in high school, she fell in love with science. While attending the University of Illinois she discovered that she also loved writing. She was fortunate to find a career that allowed her to combine both her interests. Darlene Stille has written more than 60 books for young people.